Become Unstoppable

7 Habits of Highly Successful Authors

Author Success Foundations Book 6

by

Christopher di Armani

Copyright © 2018 Christopher di Armani

All rights reserved.

https://ChristopherDiArmani.net

ISBN-13: 978-1988938110

Editor: Nicolas Johnson

Published By:
Botanie Valley Productions Inc.
PO Box 507
Lytton, BC V0K 1Z0
http://BotanieValleyProductions.com

Dedication

This book is dedicated to my sweet and loving wife Lynda. Without her unwavering support none of this would be possible.

Acknowledgments

Without the assistance of my editor, Nicolas Johnson, I can't imagine how this book would read. He tears my words apart from every conceivable angle, then offers thoughtful and constructive criticism on how best to fix the destruction at our feet. I thank God for Nicolas Johnson and his talents, daily.

#EditorsMatter

Feedback Loop

I also wish to express my heartfelt gratitude to the following individuals who took time from their own busy lives to critique this manuscript. Their willingness to assist a total stranger humbles me.

Kim Steadman (KimSteadman.com)
Sharilee Swaity (Facebook.com/Sharilee.Swaity)

Table of Contents

Foreword	1
Introduction	3
Successful Authors Write Every Day	5
Self-Discipline	5
Writer's Block Does Not Exist	6
Increase Production Daily	7
7 Simple Steps to More Words in Less Time	7
Write Even Faster	8
Drive is More Important Than Talent	8
Inspiration is for Amateurs	9
The Harder I Work the More Inspired I Am	10
Set a Daily Goal and Meet It - No Matter What	10
Build Your Writing Stamina	10
Push Yourself Beyond Your Limits	12
Successful Authors Schedule Their Writing Sessions	13
Develop a Daily Writing Schedule	13
Beginning is the Key to Writing Success	14
The Tired Cliché	14
Professionals Schedule Creativity	15
Professionals Schedule Success	15
Set Boundaries with Friends and Family	16
Successful Authors Work From Outlines	19
Outlines Breed Success	19
Outlines Breed Speed	20
Outlines Breed Creativity	20
Successful Authors Write Terrible First Drafts	23
Heed Hemingway's Advice	23

Successful Authors Set Goals and Meet Deadlines	25
Define Specific Goals	25
Manage Your Time to Achieve Those Goals	28
Track Your Progress Daily	29
Procrastination is for Pansies	29
Don't Meet Your Deadlines - Beat Them	30
Meet Specific Targets	31
Slow and Steady Wins the Race	32
Be Tenacious	32
Perseverance is Power	32
Writing Money is the Best Money	33
Self-Discipline	34
Only One Way to Finish Your Book	35
Successful Authors Focus on One Task at a Time	37
Separate Writing From Editing	37
Remove Distractions	38
Focus on One Thing at a Time	38
Relaxing Music Enhances Focus	39
Write Down Every Idea	41
Finish!	42
Successful Authors Slay Their Fears	43
Procrastination is Fear	43
Face Your Fear and Do It Anyway	43
Embrace Rejection	44
A Thick Skin is Your Best Friend	45
Believe in Yourself	46
Never Give Up on Your Dream	47
The Road to Success: Don't Lie to Yourself	48
One Last Thing	49
Books by Christopher di Armani	51

Foreword

Success leaves clues.

Figure out what successful authors did to advance their careers, then do what they did. It's the most effective course of action. Simple concept, but we must do the work. You know, the hard part.

In the pages ahead I discuss each habit as well as the lies we tell ourselves to rationalize our lack of forward progress. Finally, I shine the light of truth on the lies we tell ourselves and laugh as I watch them scurry away like little cockroaches.

I include anecdotes from my own life, where appropriate, to explain the principle at play and give you a real-world example of my successes and my failures to implement them.

Apply these principles to your life and you'll achieve their success. It's inevitable. All it takes is a pinch of perseverance, a dash of focus, and two cups of hard work.

I studied successful authors to learn how they do what they do. I examined their work ethic, their writing habits, and their life stories to find the clues they left behind. I use it all to increase my chances to achieve their success.

This book is the result. May it guide you down Publication Highway and keep you safe along the way.

Chapter 1

Introduction

Are You a Successful Author?

The Merriam-Webster Dictionary defines success as

    1. a favorable or desired outcome, and
    2. The attainment of wealth, favor, or a position of prominence or superiority.

The success you seek, your "favorable or desired outcome," is different than mine. Success, "the attainment of wealth, favor, or a position of prominence or superiority," also means something different to you than it does to me.

Some authors view financial success as the ultimate goal. For others, it's achieving "expert status" in their chosen field or earning a living doing what they love. For still others, success is holding their finished book in their hand after their long and arduous journey down Publication Highway.

However you define it, success can't arrive until you finish your book. Ask yourself the following questions and answer them honestly.

Do you review your accomplishments at the end of each day?

Do you plan what you will write tomorrow?

Are you happy with your current daily output?

Did you write your author vision statement? Are its core values reflected in your work ethic?

If you answered "No" to any of these questions, maybe it's time to follow the first rule of success: Learn what successful authors did and emulate their actions in your life.

The first four books in the Author Success Foundations series asked you to examine your current habits and beliefs and, with your honest evaluation to guide you, redesign your daily life to reflect the importance you place on finishing your book.

If you want to finish your book faster, with more productivity and less procrastination, more peace of mind and less frustration, writing more words in less time than you do today, embrace the road ahead.

Successful authors:

1. Write every day.
2. Schedule their writing sessions.
3. Work from detailed outlines.
4. Write terrible first drafts as fast as possible.
5. Set specific goals and meet their deadlines.
6. Focus on one task at a time.
7. Slay their fears and do the work anyway.

This is the path all successful and prolific writers take in their journey down Publication Highway.

You may already understand these concepts in your head, but if you do not take them into your heart and apply them to your life, success will elude you.

Open your heart, discard your hesitation and disbelief, and abandon your preconceived notions.

Adopt the seven habits of highly successful authors.

Embrace your new author mindset and use it to blaze your path down Publication Highway.

Chapter 2

Successful Authors Write Every Day

Self-Discipline

Self-discipline is the "correction or regulation of oneself for the sake of improvement."

In other words, we must do what we know we should do, when we know we should to it.

Successful writers share a common trait with other writers. Often, they don't want to sit down and write. The difference is, successful writers do it anyway.

Like any other habit, doing what we know we should do, when we should do it, is a daily challenge. Self-discipline requires we make the decision to write, each day, and follow our decision with action.

For me, this is the hard part, sitting down at my desk, opening my word processor and beginning. Writing is easy. Once I make the decision to write and follow my decision with appropriate action, the words flow, ideas bubble up from the depths of my subconscious on to the page. It's awesome.

But it all starts with a decision.

I must apply self-discipline to correct and regulate my behavior so I will sit down at my desk and write.

Despite all attempts, I still cannot find an easier way.

Writer's Block Does Not Exist

Writer's block is the single most debilitating myth ever perpetrated on creative types.

Urban myth says one writer who, upon missing his deadline (again), complained to his editor he was blocked - he had writer's block. This psychological nonsense gained immediate traction and this lazy fool gave every writer on the planet an excuse for why they don't do their job.

Writer's block is not a disease. It is not some nebulous malady without a cure.

Writer's block is, to be blunt, the bullshit excuse we toss out when we don't want to do what we know we must do, when we know we must do it. In other words, writer's block is a convenient excuse for those times we refuse to apply self-discipline to plant our butt in the chair and write.

The next time you find yourself whining, either internally or externally, "I have writer's block," do yourself a favor. Sit down, open your word processor and pound on your keyboard.

I don't care what you write. It doesn't matter. Just write. I guarantee within five minutes the words will flow from you effortlessly, like magic.

There is no magic.

We are writers, so write already. Stop making excuses for refusing to do your job. Take responsibility for your decision not to write and make a better choice.

Decide, here and now, you will write.

Nobody will do it for you, nobody can do it for you, and nobody cares if you don't finish your book, except you. Understand, deep in your soul, you and you alone are responsible for your finished book. Abandon every seductive excuse and finish your book.

Do you value yourself? Do you value your message to the world?

Do you care if you ever finish your book?

I hope and pray your answer is a heartfelt "YES!" screamed from the rooftops, before you climb back down and Just Do It.

Increase Production Daily

You can write more words per hour than you do today. The only relevant questions are:

1. Do you want to write more words per hour?
2. If yes, are you willing to do the work required to reach and maintain a higher word count every hour you write?

It sounds so simple, doesn't it? It is simple. However, just because it is simple, doing it is not easy.

I will tell you the truth, always. Yes, even when you don't want to hear it. I don't care about your unwillingness. My job, the job you "hired" me to do when you bought this book, is to be honest; to tell you the cold, hard facts and shine the light of truth on your lies.

The secret to a higher word count is practice - daily, consistent practice.

When you write every day, you do two things.

First, you build the foundation, the habit, of a successful writing career.

Second, the more you perform a task the greater your proficiency becomes.

It's inevitable.

So, the unanswered questions become:

Will you make the decision to write every day?

Will you follow your decision with the action required?

7 Simple Steps to Write More Words in Less Time

When you grant yourself permission to write fast, you unlock the door to your true capabilities. Challenge yourself. Put a clock on your writing and push yourself with these simple steps.

1. Sit down at your computer.
2. Open your word processor.
3. Set a timer for 15 minutes.
4. Start the timer.
5. Write like mad until the clock stops.
6. Record your word count.
7. Repeat steps 1 thru 6 every day for 30 days.

The purpose is to put yourself into flow - to dump as many words as possible from your mind to the page in the shortest time possible. It does not matter if the words make sense. It does not matter if the words are in the "correct" order. All that matters is you dump words on the page as fast as you possibly can.

Train your mind and your body to write fast. Give yourself permission to write with no regard to quality. This is the key to writing more words in less time. The only measure of success **for this exercise** is word count. You want to write more words every time.

If you do not have a writing timer, download my free Pomodoro Writing Timer from:

https://ChristopherDiArmani.net/free-pomodoro-writing-timer

Write Even Faster

Perform this 15-minute speed-writing challenge every day. Time of day does not matter - completing the exercise does.

Use it to wind down. Make it fun by rewarding yourself with a treat every time you break your previous record or when you achieve a particular word count milestone.

Challenge yourself to improve, to write more words faster, every week. Track your progress. If, for example, you write 300 words in 15 minutes, challenge yourself to write 350. When you achieve your target, raise it to 400. Keep raising the bar for yourself.

A friend of mine tried this test and discovered he could dump over 1,000 words on a page in 15 minutes. I almost puked. I don't achieve anything close to his word count. He managed it on his very first attempt.

So much for me being a fast writer… Back to the practice pen for me. Ignore my incessant whimpers of "I'm not worthy" as I slink away.

Drive is More Important Than Talent

No matter who you are, God gave you some measure of writing talent. How much talent is irrelevant. Yes, irrelevant. Every human being on earth is blessed with talents, but talent is not what matters.

Countless men and women, blessed with incredible minds and capacity for thought, are homeless, drive cabs or work at some other menial job. They do not use their incredible God-given gifts to achieve anything beyond paying the bills.

They lack drive.

Talent without drive is useless, as proven by the shocking lack of any real achievement by too many Mensa members.

Drive without talent is an unstoppable force. Your will, your drive to write your book, carries you far further than your writing talent, alone.

Writing is a skill. Anyone can learn a skill. Work hard every day to hone the writing talent God gave you into a mighty skill to change the world.

You can do this. I know it.

More important, you know it, too.

Inspiration is for Amateurs

"I write when I'm inspired, and I see to it that I'm inspired at nine o'clock every morning."

— Peter De Vries

Make an appointment with yourself every morning at 9 a.m. (or whatever hour works best for your schedule). At the appointed time, sit down and write, whether you are inspired or not, whether you want to write or not.

Where the body goes the mind must follow. Train yourself to show up for work. Train your body to be in your writing chair every day at the appointed hour.

Commit to these four steps, every day at the start of your scheduled writing time.

1. Sit down at computer.
2. Open word processor.
3. Write gibberish, if you must, until the words make sense.
4. Do this every single day.

"Inspiration is wonderful when it happens, but the writer must develop an approach for the rest of the time."

— Leonard Bernstein

The Harder I Work the More Inspired I Am

"People on the outside think there's something magical about writing, that you go up in the attic at midnight and cast the bones and come down in the morning with a story, but it isn't like that. You sit in back of the typewriter and you work, and that's all there is to it."

— Harlan Ellison

Inspiration exists, but it must find you working. Or, as one particularly amusing author said, your muse is a tramp. Slap handcuffs on the bitch and chain her to your desk. Don't let her go until your manuscript is done.

Inspiration is the reward for hard work.

The harder I work, the more inspired I become.

Go figure.

Set a Daily Goal and Meet It - No Matter What

Set a clear goal for yourself, the more specific the better.

I will write 500 words in 1 hour.

I will write 2,000 words before lunch.

Change the number to suit your current ability, then strive to achieve your goal, no matter what.

If your husband runs in screaming the house is on fire tell him, calmly, you will join him as soon as you finish another 300 words. Yes, he will rant and rave like a lunatic, but ignore him. Your word count matters; the flames licking at the doorway do not.

They'll wait for you. The flames, at least, understand the importance of daily success. Your spouse clearly does not.

Build Your Writing Stamina

Writing a book is like training for a marathon. You do not run 26 miles the day after you decide you want to run the Boston Marathon. You train for months, if not years, to build up your endurance.

Writing a book is no different.

You can't write 5,000 words per day tomorrow just because you decided you would do so, today. You must practice. You must train. You must improve your skills.

It is not easy to sit in one spot for three hours. It requires self-discipline. It requires single-minded focus on the task at hand to draw the magic out of your mind and ease it down on the page in front of you.

When I exhort you to build your writing stamina, I mean:

1. Work every day to increase your hourly word count.
2. Increase the number of minutes you write, if only by 1 minute per day.

Manuscript Math says when you increase your hourly word count and increase the time you write, you put more words on paper.

Simple.

Keep pushing your limits to see if they are real. Most of the time, limits are illusions, fabrications of the mind used to rationalize your mediocre word count.

Smash them. They only hold you back.

You will write more words in less time a month from now than you write today. You will write more words in less time six months from now than you will thirty days from today.

When I could barely write 500 words per day, writing 5,000 words in a single day felt impossible.

I thought the people who claimed such nonsense were liars.

One day I wrote 5,000 words.

Then I did it again.

And again.

Now, it's routine. In fact, if I do not write 5,000 words in a day I think it's a failure. I expect large word counts and am disappointed when I fall short of those expectations.

Believe it is possible. Work hard to turn your belief into reality. To sound like a corny self-help guru for a moment, believe and you will achieve, guaranteed.

Information is power.

Use a timer to track your writing sessions and a spreadsheet to track your word counts.

Set a ludicrous target. Take your current daily word count and multiply it by five - no, multiply it by ten - then strive every day until you hit your target.

You will achieve it. All it takes is your belief it is possible.

Decide how you will reward yourself when you reach your goal. Make it amazing. Increasing your output by a factor of 10 is no small achievement, and nor should the reward for accomplishing this awesome feat.

Push Yourself Beyond Your Limits

No matter how many words you write today, you possess the capacity to write more.

Challenge yourself. Push yourself beyond your limits. They exist in your mind, nowhere else.

FOCUS.

> Follow.
>
> One.
>
> Course.
>
> Until.
>
> Successful.

Dare yourself to double your daily word count. Bet against yourself and make it count. Make the bet so big you cannot afford to lose.

Then get to work.

Chapter 3

Successful Authors Schedule Their Writing Sessions

Develop a Daily Writing Schedule

"The one ironclad rule is that I have to try. I have to walk into my writing room and pick up my pen every weekday morning."
— Anne Tyler

Consistency, not inspiration, breeds success. The more you write, the more you want to write. It's an amazing, self-fulfilling cycle.

The most powerful tool to improve your output is a writing schedule. No matter your life's circumstances, you can carve out 15 minutes to write at some point in your day. Yes, even if you work 14 hours a day and are married, with five children.

It all comes down to a single question.

Will I write today?

The only acceptable answer is "Yes," so how will you make time to write?

Examine your life. Cut out every non-essential activity and spend those precious minutes writing.

You want to write a book?

Prove it. Schedule time to write every day. Then keep those appointments with destiny, for they *are* your destiny.

You do believe in destiny, don't you?

Beginning is the Key to Writing Success

Writing is easy. Starting to write is hard.

Do whatever it takes to plant your butt in the chair in front of your computer.

Lie to yourself, if necessary, like I do. When procrastination rears its ugly head, I grab my writing timer and set it for ten minutes. I lie to myself. I tell myself I must write for ten minutes, then I can quit.

The beauty of the lie is it works. In a few short minutes I am so immersed in writing, I forget about the timer. I also forget about quitting in ten minutes.

I need to fire up my writing engine. Once it's started, it does the rest. If lying to myself is what it takes to motivate me, I'm good with the deception.

I'll forgive myself later, I promise.

The Tired Cliché

"I'm too tired to write."

No, you're too lazy to write. There's a difference. Harsh? Perhaps, but I told you at the outset my job is to be honest. I'm not about to lie to you now, not about this pathetic and hackneyed cliché.

Remember what I said earlier? Starting is the hard part. Writing is easy.

I make you this iron-clad guarantee. Within three minutes, you will be wide awake, totally focused, and 100% absorbed in your story, if you just sit down at your computer and begin.

I make this guarantee with total confidence because this is my experience, every single time. Every. Single. Time.

Here's the fun part. Hours later, when I fall into bed, physically exhausted and mentally drained, I practically glow with a sense of accomplishment.

It's awesome, and I sleep great. Bonus points.

Try it. I dare you to prove me wrong.

Did you catch that?

I threw a gauntlet at your feet. You gonna pick it up? Or will you just stand there and glare at me like somehow it's *my* fault you aren't writing?

Professionals Schedule Creativity

The timeless maxim "if it doesn't get scheduled, it doesn't get done" is cliché because it is true. Professional writers set aside blocks of time, every day, to write. Professional writers schedule their creativity. During this time, they write. Everything else can wait.

This is not the time for research. This is not the time for editing. This is not the time to reread your previous day's work and pat yourself on the back for a job well done.

This is *creative* time. This is *writing* time. If you need to research a fact, make a note in the margin and keep going.

Schedule time to write. Keep your appointment and write. Make this your iron-clad rule.

Your finished manuscript will thank you for your diligence, determination and self-discipline.

Professionals Schedule Success

Professional writers schedule their success. Shelley Hitz, author, coach and founder of *Author Audience Academy*, challenges her members to set a 90-day goal. Each week throughout those 90 days, Shelley and her merry band of accomplices work hard and hold each other accountable to achieve those goals.

But it goes far deeper than holding each other accountable. Shelley asks each participant to make a commitment, both to themselves and to the group, to achieve their goal. She asks each person to fill in a Certificate of Commitment and post it on the wall of their writing room.

This Certificate of Commitment is a daily reminder of a promise made, a promise to be honored.

Simple? Absolutely.

This certificate taps into our integrity. We *want* to keep our word. We want to honor our commitments and we feel bad when we don't.

Break your goal into as many pieces as possible, then schedule each one on your calendar.

This is your roadmap to success. Just follow the road.

Set Boundaries With Friends and Family

Decide writing time is valuable, then protect your most precious asset. Nobody else will take you seriously until you take your commitment seriously.

The least favorite word in the English language is "No."

This tiny word is the key to boundaries with your spouse, your kids, and anyone else who wants to infringe upon the time you set aside to write. Setting a goal is one thing, setting boundaries to achieve your dream is a very different animal.

When I quit my full-time job to write, I'd be lying if I said it was easy.

First, I needed to overcome my own innate desire to procrastinate. It took months. Once I beat that demon into submission, I needed to deal with my wife's desire to spend all day with me.

At first, my wife interrupted me a lot. She wanted to make up for lost time, now that I didn't work 80+ hours per week.

I loved seeing her so happy, but between my own procrastination issues and her constantly dropping in to talk, I found it almost impossible to accomplish anything.

We needed a system to balance both needs - her need to spend quality time with her husband and my need to write every day.

If I wanted time to write each day, and I did, my wife and I needed to establish clear boundaries.

On my side, the boundary became, "If my office door is closed, I am not to be disturbed."

On her side, the limit was, "Your door can't stay closed all day."

This produced an interesting side effect, both in my life and in our marriage.

When my office door is closed, I must write. I feel an urgency to get the job done. Otherwise, my closed door disrespects both my wife and my commitment to her.

On her side, she respects my door is only closed when necessary and she honors my writing time. She leaves me alone.

Her interruptions challenged me to become focused and committed.

The moment my wife realized I was serious about my commitment to write, her resistance melted away.

In short, both our needs are met.

I close the door when I need time to write without interruption, but leave it open otherwise. I take breaks to visit with her, to take a walk, and share what we're going through each day.

Challenging, to begin with, but ultimately far more rewarding for each of us individually, and for our marriage.

Chapter 4

Successful Authors Work From Outlines

Outlines Breed Success

"Structure is important. Know your ending before you start writing. You wouldn't just get into your car and drive without knowing where you're going. Know your most important plot points. This does not mean things won't change, but you will never get stuck."

— Peter James

Successful authors work from detailed outlines.

Why? An outline is your road map. It is your guide to your destination - your completed manuscript.

But it's more than a road map. It's every decision you made through each twist and turn of Publication Highway.

An example from Lewis Carroll's *Alice's Adventures in Wonderland* explains why an outline is necessary.

> "Cheshire Puss," Alice began, rather timidly, as she did not know whether it would like the name: however, it only grinned a little wider. "Would you tell me, please, which way I ought to go from here?"
>
> "That depends a good deal on where you want to get to," said the Cat.
>
> "I don't much care where," said Alice.
>
> "Then it doesn't matter which way you go," said the Cat.

The effort required to make sound decisions depletes your mind's energy and your willpower. It decreases your ability to make sound decisions later in the day.

An outline removes those decisions from the process of writing and frees you to do what you do best, write.

Creating an outline is a process filled with decisions. This is why we dislike them. An outline is hard work and, at heart, most writers are lazy. Allow me to rephrase. I should not presume to speak for you. Creating an outline is hard work and, at heart, *I* am lazy.

Better?

I love to write but I am lazy. There, I said it.

I want to write as fast and easy as possible. As a result of my inherent laziness, I've tried everything, and I mean everything, to find an easier way.

Writing an outline is the easier way.

For me.

I write faster from a detailed outline.

I write higher quality words, sentences and paragraphs, because I remove the need to think from the equation.

I despise the outline process. It is neither fun nor pleasurable. I find it painful, excruciating, at times.

While I realize my experience is the result of my own value judgments, I admit I am not yet ready to let go of those judgments. Yes, even though I know the only person I hurt by hanging on to them is me.

My mind will believe anything, literally anything I tell it, so why do I insist on filling it with this garbage about how difficult it is to create an outline? Because I am a frail and pathetic human being. I love to hang on to bad ideas even though I realize they impede my progress.

Despite my bad attitude, I love what a detailed outline does for me. I never worry about what to write. No need. I decided "what" to write ages ago, when I constructed my outline.

All that remains now are the fun bits - writing and editing - and I love the fun bits.

Outlines Breed Speed

Writing from a detailed outline is also the fastest way to write. With no decisions to make about plot, character or story, every ounce of my creative being is focused and I pour the story from of my mind to the page. It's glorious.

During NaNoWriMo 2017, I wrote 50,000 words in 10 days (my personal best) and near the end of the month I wrote another 20,000 words in three days. In the process I blew my mind.

How I felt at the end of those three days shocked me, not the massive word count. I expected to feel tired and beat up. Instead, I felt calm, refreshed and ready for more.

Outlines Breed Creativity

The Plotter vs. Pantser Wars are absurd.

Every writer on the planet is both Plotter and Pantser.

I can't write when I don't know what to write about, nor can you.

I cannot immerse myself in a scene and deliver all the passion and fury it requires until I write the scene.

No amount of planning on earth gets me there. It all comes out in the moment, as the scene comes to life before my eyes.

Every writer must plan.

Every writer must also fly by the seat of their pants.

A detailed outline does not, I repeat not, destroy your creativity. It does the opposite. It opens the floodgates and allows your creativity to flow like a raging river.

When you remove the hard decisions about plot, character and story from your sessions, you free yourself to write with abandon.

The difference between you and me is the degree your personality favors one over the other.

Some writers need an extraordinary level of detail in their outlines. Others require a single sheet of paper with the barest sketch of chapter breakdowns.

Both bring their creative power to bear on writing.

Make writing easy.

Build your outline.

If there was an easier way, I would use it.

I'm lazy, remember?

This *is* the easy way.

Chapter 5

Successful Authors Write Terrible First Drafts

Heed Hemingway's Advice

Ernest Hemingway said, "The first draft of anything is shit."

Anne Lamott took it a step farther. She exhorts us to write "shitty first drafts" on purpose.

> "All good writers write them. This is how they end up with good second drafts and terrific third drafts. People tend to look at successful writers, writers who are getting their books published and maybe even doing well financially, and think that they sit down at their desks every morning feeling like a million dollars, feeling great about who they are and how much talent they have and what a great story they have to tell… Not one of them writes elegant first drafts."

Take their advice to heart.

The day I allowed myself to write lousy first drafts is the same day my word count exploded.

Once I grasped the fact nobody would ever read my first draft, its quality became irrelevant.

What a life-altering realization.

I don't write crappy first drafts any more.

Sure, I must reorder my thoughts into a coherent and logical order, but I know I'll change my mind about that half a dozen times before I publish, so why get my knickers in a twist over it while writing the first draft?

I love writing fast. I turn it into a game. I reward myself for milestones, like the silly gold stars on my calendar. Today I earned seven of those little buggers. The best part is I don't even feel like I work hard, most days.

Editing days don't count. Those are all hard work. Gratifying, of course, but hard work.

The purpose of a first draft is to puke words on the page so, when it comes time to edit, after my first draft is complete, there is a huge pile to play with.

The time for an honest assessment is later, not now, as I fill empty page after empty page with my words.

That's the beauty of "writing crap" in my first draft. When I don't place a value judgment on my words, when I remove my internal criticism, I write faster and I write better. The quality of my first drafts continue to improve, while the time required to complete them decreases.

It's brilliant!

Give yourself permission to write lousy first drafts.

It frees you from the tyranny of your Infernal Editor.

It unleashes a gushing river of creativity.

Write like the Devil himself lit your hair on fire and God refuses to put it out until you're done. Dump those words on the page as fast as you can and refuse, utterly refuse, to change a single word until your manuscript is finished.

I know I contradicted myself, just now, by going back to fix that spelling error. Don't be me. Be better than me.

Chapter 6

Successful Authors Set Goals and Meet Deadlines

Define Specific Goals

If the outline is your roadmap to success, goals are the signposts you must heed as you travel down Publication Highway.

Goals are a requirement for successful authors.

Publishing a book is a process with many component parts:

- ❑ Create your outline
- ❑ Write your book's first draft
- ❑ Edit your book
- ❑ Send it to a professional editor
- ❑ Rewrite your book based on your editing feedback
- ❑ Final edit of your book
- ❑ Design the book's cover art
- ❑ Create the book's Kindle cover art
- ❑ Create the book's Paperback cover art (front and back)
- ❑ Create your book's entry on Amazon KDP
- ❑ Create your book's entry on Createspace
- ❑ Hit the magic button on both platforms

This is an overview, obviously.

You can (and should) break each step into its smallest component parts, then assign a deadline to each one.

When you break your objective (finish and publish your book) into its component parts, you transform this daunting and seemingly unattainable goal into a series of easily-accomplished tasks.

Precision is Key

To be effective, your written goal must be:

1. Specific
2. Measurable
3. Achievable
4. Realistic
5. Time-Bound
6. Challenging

Example:

I will write 500 words per day for 30 days.

Specific

The goal is defined with precision. The desired aim or purpose is to write 500 words each day.

Measurable

Either the writer will write 500 words each day or she won't. If she does, she meets the goal. If she doesn't, she fails to meet it.

Achievable

Anyone can write 500 words per day, but the writer must commit to performing the task. He must embrace the challenge daily, not shy away from it, ever.

Realistic

Yes, it is possible for you to write 500 words per day, even if you are not yet capable of it today.

Time-Bound

Yes. The writer will accomplish this feat every day for 30 consecutive days.

Challenging

The definition of challenging depends upon you, your writing habits and current work, family and social commitments. For best results, make your goal push you out of your comfort zone.

Force yourself to stretch your writer's wings further each day.

If you write 500 words per day, pump up your daily word count to 750. If you struggle to achieve those 750 words, great. Strive to meet your goal and you will discover it becomes easy in short order. The more you confront the limits of "possible" for yourself, the more you build your writing muscles and the stronger they become.

For example, when I could write 4,000 words per day six days in a row, I raised the bar. I challenged myself to write 5,000 words per day, a goal I achieved the following week. My current goal is to write 8,000 words per day. I'm not there yet, but my goal is defined with precision, I designed a plan to achieve it, and I work every day to increase my word count.

Will I write 8,000 words per day consistently? Absolutely. There is no doubt in my mind, and this is the key. My belief 8,000 words per day is possible and achievable means I can do it, provided I put in the work required, every day, to build my writing muscles.

Only by pushing myself out of my comfort zone, beyond what I currently believe possible, will I discover my capabilities. The same is true for you.

I do, however, offer two caveats.

CAVEAT #1: Every writer is different.

What is hard for me may be simple for you, or vice versa. Never judge your accomplishments by the bar another writer sets for him or herself. Judge yourself by your accomplishments and push yourself daily to stretch beyond your personal best.

CAVEAT #2: Every writing project is different.

For one project, I could ONLY write between the hours of 10pm and 4am. Others I can only write during the day. Some I write easily, no matter the time of day (or night).

If you find it difficult to write a specific project at a specific time, walk away from it for 6 hours, then try again. Keep searching until you find the sweet spot where you write most productively for that project.

Don't be shocked if the answer you find is a little crazy, as I did, and you're writing like a demon possessed from 10 p.m. until 4 a.m. for 21 straight nights.

If it can happen to me, it just might happen to you too.

The important takeaway is this - be open to all possibilities to get your words on the page.

Manage Your Time to Achieve Those Goals

Setting goals for every step of the process is laudable, but it is futile unless you manage your time effectively to achieve them.

Once your goals are defined and you've assigned deadlines to each one, mark every deadline down on a calendar.

I use colored Post-It notes on both a desk and wall calendar. If I could find a tri-monthly calendar I liked, I'd use it so my entire 90-day goal is mapped out on the wall.

Or maybe I'll build a computer program so I can see all three months on the screen at once. You know, the next time I feel the overwhelming need to procrastinate from writing.

Each color represents a specific deadline on my road to publication. For example, yellow notes define the start date for a specific chapter. Blue notes signify a chapter's deadline. Pink notes mark the start and end of editing phases, both self-editing and professional. Purple denotes special deadlines I must meet along the way to stay on course.

This system of color-coded notes works for me.

Develop a system to schedule your time, then keep those appointments. Determine how many words you must write every day to meet your goals - weekly, monthly, etc.

Then work hard, not to meet your deadlines, but to beat them.

The most successful authors set and stick to hard publishing deadlines, just like "real" publishers. This sounds hard but, in reality, is quite simple. You just need to know two things:

1. The approximate length of your book (word count), and
2. How many words you write per hour.

Manuscript Math tells you how many days you need to write your book. If you write 500 words per hour to complete an 80,000-word book, you need 160 hours of writing time. If you write three hours per day, you will take 53 days of writing to complete your book.

What happens when you improve your word count per hour? Or write for longer each day?

Set a deadline. Make it challenging, outside of your comfort zone, then push yourself and work hard to beat your deadline.

Track Your Progress Daily

A small wall calendar hangs in front of my desk. Its sole purpose is to track my daily progress. I do not post deadlines here, only little gold stars to track my word counts.

Go to your local Dollar Store and purchase a wall calendar. While you're at the Dollar Store, grab a package of stickers, gold stars, thumbs up, whatever strikes your fancy. Hang your new calendar on the wall in front of your desk. If you write on specific days of the week, mark your schedule on the calendar first. If you write every day except Sunday, like I do, hang the calendar and get back to work.

Every day, after you achieve your target, stick a gold star to the square for today's date. I award one gold star for each 2,500 words I write per day and 1 gold star for every 5,000 words I edit during the editing phase. It's a powerful visual indicator of my productivity and consistency.

This also doubles as a reward system. I can't speak for you, but I love rewards, even if they're cheesy and I give them to myself.

For reasons I neither understand nor care to analyze, these little gold stars are a powerful motivator for me.

Try it.

You may discover, to your delight, how useful this silly reward can be, and how important it becomes, psychologically, to build an unbroken string of gold stars on your calendar.

Procrastination is for Pansies

The title of this section may offend some readers. If it offends you, it's probably because procrastination is an issue for you, as it is for me. Take a deep breath, exhale your indignation and read on.

Procrastination is the slayer of your dreams. It's the serial killer of everything good in your life. It slaughters your dreams without hesitation or the slightest regard for your feelings. (Much like the title of this section, I suppose.)

Procrastination is your refusal to write, even though you know you should.

Every human being shares one fatal character flaw. We don't like doing what we know we should do, when we should do it, to achieve success.

This is every bit as true for successful authors as it is for unpublished ones. Where successful authors differ is this: they employ self-discipline to write even when they would rather do something else, something more enjoyable instead.

Their willingness to delay gratification in the short term is embodied in the phrase "short term pain for long term gain."

Whether we label it self-discipline, self-control, self-denial or delayed gratification, the end result is the same. Successful authors do what they should do, when they should do it, whether they feel like it or not.

So, will you write today?

You can either make excuses or you can make progress toward your goal.

The choice is yours.

Don't Meet Your Deadlines - Beat Them

Successful authors don't meet deadlines, they beat them.

A deadline is the latest you can achieve your goal. Miss this and you are a failure - so don't miss it.

Set deadlines to challenge your abilities, then work your butt off to beat them.

Build a mindset where your minimum expectation is to achieve your goal by its deadline. If you meet your deadline, you should feel just a little unsatisfied, disappointed even. Sure, you achieved your goal, but so what? You already knew you would.

Strive to beat your goals, every time.

If your goal is to write your first draft in 60 days, fight hard to complete it in 55 days instead. When you do, it means two things.

First, you challenged yourself and not only did you rise to the challenge, you also met it head on and won.

Second, you just added five extra days to your editing cycle, where you need every minute you can find.

If your goal is to publish one book this year, work like a crazy person to publish two, instead. Continually challenge yourself to beat your goals and you will write more, write faster, write better, and publish more work every year.

Turn the challenge of beating your deadline into a daily success habit.

If your goal is to write 1,000 words in an hour, can you write them in 55 minutes instead? How about 50?

Challenge yourself.

You will discover you are capable of far more than you believe today.

Meet Specific Targets

Goals are wonderful and required, but there are many ways to challenge yourself to write faster.

Set specific targets for your daily, weekly and monthly word count goals. Figure out a way to treat yourself and deny those treats until you achieve these targets. Figure out what you love and turn it into a reward.

Sour cream and onion potato chips are my Kryptonite.

If a bag exists in my home, I sniff it out and devour it, without mercy or hesitation. It's terrible.

Since they are detrimental to my overall health, I don't allow myself to eat them regularly. Instead, I turn my weakness for potato chips into a reward.

Whenever I publish a new book I reward myself with a bag of chips and a Pepsi. I deny myself *unless and until I earn them.*

While this may not work for you, it is one of a series of games I play with myself to write faster, write better and publish more books. This does NOT mean I skimp on quality. Not for one second. Every word I publish is a reflection of me, of my abilities and my professionalism.

I guard my writing reputation diligently and refuse to publish substandard work. Is my work perfect? Not a chance. It is, however, the very best work I can deliver at the time.

I love writing fast. I believe the purpose of a first draft is to vomit as many words on the page as possible, in as short a time as I can. Only then can I turn all my barnyard swill into something worthy of publication.

And when I do, I reward myself with the biggest bag of chips I can find, and chase them down my gullet with a bucket of Pepsi.

Yes… I know… much room for improvement, but if you think I'm terrible now, imagine me *before* God put His mitts on me.

Slow and Steady Wins the Race

While the rabbit ran fast for short periods of time, the tortoise won the race because of his relentless pursuit of the finish line.

Writing is no different. Set an achievable word count goal and relentlessly pursue this target. Meet your goal every day. This is a far more productive path to a completed manuscript than writing a ton of words today, then not another word for the rest of the week because you're so wiped out.

You enhance your skills and abilities faster. Over time, your achievable daily word count increases, as does the skill with which you write those words.

There is power in the work ethic of the tortoise. Use it. Pursue your dream. Write with diligence every day. You'll pass a lot of sleeping rabbits along the way, writers without a published book to their name, while you publish more books year in, year out.

Be the tortoise.

Be Tenacious

Tenacity is your ability to persist until you achieve something valued or desired. It's the ability to fight to accomplish your objective, to never give up your dream, to give everything to realize your goal.

Your dream of a published book is a flight of fancy unless you take concrete action to transform your dream into reality. This transformation occurs with work, lots of hard work, and your determination to see it through to the end.

Self-discipline is your friend. Use it. Every day.

Perseverance Is Power

The Merriam-Webster Dictionary defines perseverance as *continued effort to do or achieve something despite difficulties, failure, or opposition.*

Procrastination is your biggest enemy but you must defeat others as you travel down Publication Highway.

Jobs, your spouse or significant other, children, relatives, friends and sports all demand your most precious commodity - time.

Apply self-discipline to finish your book.

Schedule time to write and defend it ruthlessly. Overcome every obstacle until your manuscript is complete.

Those little gold stars I reward myself with each day are a record, if you will, of my persistence, of my tenacity. They are proof I did what I said I would do, when I said I would do it, whether I felt like it or not.

When I look at my calendar (impossible to avoid - it hangs right above my computer screen) and see my unbroken string of gold stars, I get downright belligerent. I refuse to break the chain.

I write, even though I don't want to.

That's powerful mojo for a pack of stickers from the dollar store.

I will use every tool in my toolbox to motivate myself and complete my manuscript. Some days are easy. Some are nightmarishly difficult. Some days I battle internal demons, other days I battle the expectations of others.

The internal conflict takes place daily, at least for me. With perseverance, you will survive the war. No, not survive. You will win the war.

Simple but not easy, remember?

Writing Money is the Best Money

If someone pays you to write, no matter how much or how little, think back to the first time they paid you for your words. If you're like me, the thought makes you giddy with joy.

"Writing money is the BEST money."

You might think I'd get tired of saying it, but I don't. My wife laughs at me, every time.

Whenever someone pays me for writing, it's like Christmas. I did the one thing I love to do most in this world, and someone gave me money for it.

Honestly, does it get any better?

Write everything.

Write for anyone willing to pay you cold, hard cash.

Take a moment to rejoice in it, then get back to work.

The next paycheck cannot arrive until you finish your current job.

Self-Discipline

Brian Tracy, in his book *No Excuses! The Power of Self-Discipline*, discusses how character is defined by our willingness to do what is necessary to ensure success, even when we don't want to.

> The only bulwark against temptation, the path of least resistance, and the expediency factor is character. The only way that you can develop your full character is by exerting your willpower in every situation when you are tempted to do what is easy and expedient rather than what is correct and necessary.[1]

Proper systems, such as a pre-determined structure for your writing day, ensure success with one important caveat - you must implement the plan contained within its structure.

Do I want to write for three hours every day?

If this week is any example, my own answer is a clear and resounding "NO!"

I would rather do anything except write, but I also know my current work in progress, the book you now hold in your hands, will not complete itself.

Despite my own struggles with self-discipline, I continue to write every day because I also understand the immense satisfaction I will experience when I'm finished.

This delayed gratification is my objective and, while my editor says I'm a prolific writer, my own experience is quite different.

He sees only the completed projects as they land on his desk.

I see the daily struggle to do those things I know I must do, when I must do them, whether I want to do them or not.

I also know the immense joy I will feel when an author, perhaps even you, writes to tell me how this book changed their life or how it gave them the tools to finish their book.

That joy is only possible when I use my self-discipline to get the job done, even when I don't want to.

So far, it's working.

Only One Way to Finish Your book

Nobody will write your book as well as you.

Nobody else will write your book, period.

There is only one way to finish your manuscript. Sit down every day and write. You will not find a better, easier or faster way to write your book.

So why are you still here reading this page? Why aren't you seated at your desk pounding on the keyboard until your eyes glaze over and your fingers bleed?

What? Are you waiting for *me* to write it?

Good luck with that!

Chapter 7

Successful Authors Focus on One Task at a Time

Separate Writing from Editing

Never edit when you write.

Never write when you edit.

Sound advice.

The purpose of your first draft is to vomit words on the page so, when it comes time to edit, you have big piles of words to work with.

When your first draft is complete, then and only then, allow your Infernal Editor to rip your hard work to shreds.

Force the little bastard to wait a few weeks, if you can.

That will teach him for trying to mess up all those writing sessions.

For those who need rules to live by, here are three:

Writing Time is for writing.

Editing Time is for editing.

Never confuse one with the other.

Remove Distractions

FOCUS.
> Follow.
> One.
> Course.
> Until.
> Successful.

When you focus on one goal to the exclusion of all else, you will make incredible progress. The easiest way to focus on a single task is to remove all others from view. This means the following:

1. Close the door of your writing room.

My door has a sign on it - "Novelist At Work. Do Not Disturb."

2. Turn off your phone.

If you cannot bring yourself to shut down the device, turn on Airplane mode or turn off audio and visual notifications and place it face-down on your desk.

3. Turn off your Internet connection.

If you can't bring yourself to shut off the Internet tap, close your web browser and email program. Facebook can wait. So can Twitter and email.

When you begin your daily session, make sure you actually write every minute you scheduled to write.

When the dreaded Demon of Procrastination leans over your shoulder and whispers his filthy thoughts into your ear, type faster and send him straight back to Hell, where he belongs.

Focus on One Thing at a Time

The Pomodoro Technique, developed by Francesco Cirillo in the 1980s, splits your work into 25-minute sessions, each followed by a 5-minute break. Pomodoro is the Italian word for tomato, and his system is named for the tomato-shaped kitchen timer Cirillo used as a university student.

The Pomodoro Technique is the most powerful focus technique I've ever used. The system is breathtaking in its simplicity.

Pick one task.

Start the timer.

Work on it for 25 minutes. Do nothing else until the session is over.

Apply this principle to your writing and blow your mind with what you can achieve. When you focus on a single task, 25 minutes flies. It puts you under the pressure of a deadline and, if your brain is wired like mine, it is a powerful way to pry the words out of my brain and dump them on the screen in front of me.

Here are two free timers. The first is a web browser-based version, and the second is a Windows program I wrote for myself. (I was a computer programmer in a previous incarnation of my life.)

https://tomato-timer.com/

https://christopherdiarmani.net/free-pomodoro-writing-timer

Relaxing Music Enhances Focus

Would you believe listening to classical music, ambient piano sounds or Gregorian Chant increases your word count? I sure didn't. Not until I tried it for a week. The results shocked me. Not only did I write more words per session, I also felt less mentally exhausted afterward.

I'm a writer. Sitting at my desk in silence while I pound out a story is what I do. It's normal. I still forget to turn on music and, as I write this sentence I realize that I, once again, forgot to take my own advice. Here I sit, working in silence.

One moment please, while I put the music on.

There… much better. I spent decades writing in silence, so it took time to break my silence habit and, as today proves one more time, I still forget more often than I like. I find instrumental piano, Gregorian Chant or my latest obsession, Costa Rican Howler Monkeys, particularly effective.

My love of Howler Monkeys in the rain is supported by a Business Insider article[2] that says you can boost your mood and enhance your focus by adding a natural sound element to your environment. My anecdotal evidence is backed up by serious research, I discovered, and offers far more benefits than an increased daily word count.

For example, French university research published in Learning and Individual Differences,[3] found that students who listened to a one-hour lecture where classical music was played in the background scored significantly higher in a quiz on the lecture when compared to a similar group of students who heard the lecture with no music.

Reader's Digest[4] reported classical music offered a host of benefits to the listener, including lower blood pressure, better sleep, boosted brain power and better memory. The Reader's Digest article cited a number of studies to back up their claims.

A 2007 Standford University School of Medicine study[5] found music moves the brain to pay attention and helps it sort incoming information.

> The Stanford University School of Medicine research team showed that music engages the areas of the brain involved with paying attention, making predictions and updating the event in memory. Peak brain activity occurred during a short period of silence between musical movements - when seemingly nothing was happening.

> In this foundational study, the researchers conclude that dynamic changes seen in the fMRI scans reflect the brain's evolving responses to different phases of a symphony. An event change - the movement transition signaled by the termination of one movement, a brief pause, followed by the initiation of a new movement - activates the first network, called the ventral fronto-temporal network. Then a second network, the dorsal fronto-parietal network, turns the spotlight of attention to the change and, upon the next event beginning, updates working memory.

> "The study suggests one possible adaptive evolutionary purpose of music," said Jonathan Berger, PhD, associate professor of music and a musician who is another co-author of the study. Music engages the brain over a period of time, he said, and the process of listening to music could be a way that the brain sharpens its ability to anticipate events and sustain attention.

Amisha Padnani, writing in the New York Times, echoed the results of these studies.[6]

> In biological terms, melodious sounds help encourage the release of dopamine in the reward area of the brain, as would eating a delicacy,

looking at something appealing or smelling a pleasant aroma, said Dr. Amit Sood, a physician of integrative medicine with the Mayo Clinic.

Dr. Lesiuk's research focuses on how music affects workplace performance.

In one study involving information technology specialists, she found that those who listened to music completed their tasks more quickly and came up with better ideas than those who didn't, because the music improved their mood.

"When you're stressed, you might make a decision more hastily; you have a very narrow focus of attention," she said. "When you're in a positive mood, you're able to take in more options."

While Costa Rican Howler Monkeys may not be your thing, listening to these amazing critters roar sends me straight to my happy place. If you want to hear them, drop me a request and I'll send you the MP3 file. You may find it's just the thing when you need a break from classical music or your own go-to audio backdrop.

https://ChristopherDiArmani.net/howler-monkeys-mp3

Write Down Every Idea

Ideas fly at us from every angle, usually at the most inopportune times. Call it the benefit or nightmare of being a creative person. The ideas never stop. This is problematic when writing. It breaks your focus.

The answer, I learned, is not to ignore those ideas when they so rudely interrupt my writing session, it's to write them down immediately. My brain is satisfied. It knows its latest brilliant thought is not lost. This allows me to get right back to work without the annoying little voice in the back of my mind whispering,

"This is important. You're going to forget me..."

Put a notepad and pen beside your bed. Put a notepad and pen beside you when you write. Carry a notepad and pen with you everywhere.

Write down at least 10 new ideas every day. Turn it into a game to see how many new ideas you can come up with. Above all, train yourself to get right back to work the second your new idea is on paper. Focus.

Finish!

Schedules, outlines, goals and deadlines are wonderful, but they are only tools. They are not the road. They help you travel down the road.

Finish your manuscript.

Nothing else matters.

You must finish your manuscript. At the end of the day, that's the reason you're here, isn't it? To learn how to finish?

Successful authors finish what they start. They complete their manuscripts. They edit their manuscripts. They pass them off to other professionals for further improvement. Then they publish.

DONE IS BETTER THAN PERFECT.
You cannot edit what you do not write.
You cannot publish what you do not complete.

I created a poster with those three sentences, added a cute graphic, then printed a dozen copies. I hung them everywhere I write.

On the windows of my office.

On the wall behind me.

Above the mirror in the bathroom.

At my writing retreat in Washington State.

The goal of every writer is to finish, then publish, so get back to your desk and complete the next chapter of your book. Move yourself one step further down Publication Highway.

I said stop reading this book and write.

What?

Was I unclear?

Chapter 8

Successful Authors Slay Their Fears

Procrastination is Fear

Procrastination is fear on steroids. Fear is never real. It's imagined, like the Bogeyman or Jason in *Friday the 13th*. It still stops us in our tracks with stunning regularity.

I can fritter a day away without writing a single word easier than any writer in history. If they held an Olympic event for procrastination, I'd win the Gold medal. Despite this, my editor calls me one of the most prolific writers he's ever known.

I laugh every time. It's true from his perspective, but my own subjective view is so different.

I wage a battle to get started every day. The question I must answer is this:

What do I fear that keeps me from writing?

So far, I lack the courage to answer.

Maybe I'll just write more, instead.

Face Your Fear and Do It Anyway

Writers live with myriad fears. Fear of success, fear of failure, fear we're lousy writers, fear we have nothing to say and should quit now, before we embarrass ourselves in front of the world.

Every one of those statements is pure, unadulterated garbage.

Every.

Single.

One.

When your own resistance bogs you down, ask yourself these questions:

1. Is this goal reasonable and achievable in the time frame I've assigned it?
2. What is distracting me from achieving my goal?
3. What internal resistance is preventing me from completing these tasks?
4. What is preventing me from writing in this moment?

Fear of success stops most writers in their tracks, me included. After I achieved some small measure of success, this particular fear is no longer my most pressing one. On the downside, other fears happily jumped in and took its place.

I'm a member of a couple writer's groups on Facebook, and in one of those groups a young woman shared her fear over publishing her first book. Her primary fear was of failure, fear nobody would read her book.

I asked her, "Who is reading your book now?"

"Nobody," came her timid reply.

"What is there to be afraid of?" I asked. "Nobody's reading your book right now. You're already living your worst-case scenario, so if just one person buys your book, that's an improvement, right?"

She published her book the next day.

Only by facing our fears do we learn if they are real.

They seldom are.

Embrace Rejection

"By the time I was fourteen the nail in my wall would no longer support the weight of the rejection slips impaled upon it. I replaced the nail with a spike and went on writing."

— Stephen King

Rejection is not the "No" we perceive it to be. Rejection means you have more to learn. It's God's gentle whisper in your ear, saying, "Not yet."

Until you quit, everything else is practice. You only fail when you stop trying. Ask any world champion and, regardless of their chosen sport, they will tell you the same thing - they learned far more from their failures than they did from success.

When you win a gold medal, it's easy to forget the many flaws in your performance. When you don't win that prize, every flaw is magnified in your mind.

There is a middle ground, where our willingness to learn, to improve, is the purpose of life. When revered masters like Hemingway say, "We are all apprentices in a craft where no one ever becomes a master," it takes a special arrogance to believe we cannot improve our craft.

A Thick Skin is Your Best Friend

The Merriam-Webster Dictionary defines criticize as "to consider the merits and demerits of and judge accordingly."

For writers, criticism comes in many forms. The content of our work is judged based in its merits on many levels. Is it well written? Is the story well crafted? Are the characters compelling and flawed?

The art of dealing with criticism is to, first and foremost, separate your writing from your personality.

When someone criticizes your work, understand they are not judging who you are as a human being, but the quality of the words you put on the page.

Once you separate who you are from what you do, handling criticism is much easier. I do not say it becomes easier to hear. Far from it. When we remove ourselves from the equation and examine the harsh words of others, we must ask ourselves hard questions in return.

Is there merit to their criticism? If so, what can I learn from their analysis, however harshly worded it may be.

If there is merit, consider this as a sign you must learn new skills or hone your existing skills. If there is no merit, ignore them entirely.

The trick, of course, is knowing the difference.

Believe In Yourself

When we answer the question, "What do you do for a living?" with "I'm a writer," the look of disdain in the eyes of the questioner is as predictable as the sneer on their face.

Until we achieve fame and fortune and accolades from an outside entity, nobody takes us seriously. Until that day arrives, we must take ourselves seriously.

We must believe in ourselves. Nobody else will - not until they view us "successful" by someone else's standards.

Once Upon a Time in Mexico, the 2003 movie written, directed and edited by Robert Rodriguez, includes one of my favourite lines of all time, delivered by Johnny Depp to a doubtful Danny Trejo.

It's hilarious because the sentiment expresses, to me, what it takes to be a writer.

"Are you a MexiCAN or a MexiCAN'T?"

"I'm a MexiCAN."

"Good."

I believe I can. I believe I can write well. I believe I can complete my books and publish them for all the world to enjoy.

Terrifying, of course, yet exhilarating, too.

When I embrace my fears and challenge them to see if they are real (they never are) and push through them, I accomplish my goals.

When we believe in ourselves and act in accordance with that belief, we scream a powerful truth out into the universe.

I WILL NOT BE DENIED.

How cool is that?

Now.

Grab a duffel bag.

Stuff all your fears inside and toss it on the bonfire.

We'll warm our hands on the flames while it burns and discuss our next writing project.

Never Give Up On Your Dream

"Long ago, I realized that success leaves clues, and that people who produce outstanding results do specific things to create those results. I believed that if I precisely duplicated the actions of others, I could reproduce the same quality of results that they had."

— Anthony Robbins

You can make excuses or you can make progress. The choice is yours.

You cannot accomplish your dream unless, until, you take action designed to move you one step closer, every day.

Goals are dreams with deadlines.

Sound advice.

Heed it.

Work hard, every single day, until your lofty dream becomes your everyday practical reality.

This reward is worth every ounce of pain you suffer on your journey down Publication Highway.

The Road to Success: Don't Lie to Yourself

The purpose of the Author Success Foundations series is to provide the tools and materials to patch those holes, to reinforce and strengthen our armor. The day of battle is here, and we must march ever forward. If we stop, even for a moment, our words will shrink under the oppressive heat of our fears and we fail.

In the seventh book in the Author Success Foundations series, I dissect seven lies writers tell ourselves and shine the light of truth upon each one.

Every lie we use to deceive ourselves obscures a truth we refuse to face. The job of a writer, any writer, is to face our fears head on, protected by the body armor of honesty, certainty and integrity. Only then can the brilliance we etch on the page shine bright for the world to see.

Each fallacy we project on ourselves corrodes holes in our armor, holes the insidious demons of worry, self-doubt, procrastination and perfectionism slip through to poison us.

Step inside. Face your fears. Show them you will not be cowed by these pathetic demons. Own your internal dialog and reshape it into a powerful and productive engine, then drive it to the end of Publication Highway.

Read the seventh book in the Author Success Foundations series, *I Don't Have Time To Write And Other Lies Writers Tell Themselves*, where I dispel the myths and lies that hold us back.

Available from your favorite online book retailers today.

For more information, visit:

https://ChristopherDiArmani.net/no-time-to-write

One Last Thing!

First, thank you for reading this book!

If you enjoyed this book and found it informative (and even if you did not) I would be grateful if you would post an honest review on Amazon and/or Goodreads. Every review helps this book find more readers, the lifeblood of any author.

https://ChristopherDiArmani.net/review-unstoppable-author-gr

https://ChristopherDiArmani.net/review-unstoppable-author-amazon

Your support in the form of an honest review really does make a difference. Reviews help authors sell more books and I read every one as part of my efforts to make my books even better.

I would also be grateful if you shared a link to this book on your social media accounts.

If, for some reason, you did not like this book or didn't get what you expected out of it please tell me directly. I will use your constructive criticism to fix any flaws in my book so it better meets your expectations. Please contact me here:

https://ChristopherDiArmani.net/Contact

Thank you so much for your support, feedback and your honest reviews.

Sincerely,

Christopher di Armani

Author Extraordinare

http://ChristopherDiArmani.net/Books

About Christopher di Armani

"Author Extraordinaire"

Christopher di Armani is an Amazon bestselling author and the creator of Author Success Foundations.

This 7-book series teaches authors at any level how to develop the mindset, daily routines and work habits necessary to unleash their creativity and get their books published.

Christopher has published 16 books and produced 4 documentary films on topics ranging from the craft of writing to civil liberties and politics.

Books by Christopher

Awaken Your Author Mindset: Finish Writing Your Book Fast (Author Success Foundations 1)

https://ChristopherDiArmani.net/author-mindset

https://ChristopherDiArmani.net/author-mindset-workbook

Learn how to develop your bullet-proof Author Mindset and create a system guaranteed to deliver success and to build the habits required to work this system every single day.

The choice is yours. If you continue to do what you've always done you'll just get what you already have, an unfinished manuscript and all the disappointment, discarded dreams and self-loathing you can handle.

You will never finish your book.

Now, imagine the possible…

Allow me to be your guide to help you construct a mindset, a solid foundation to complete your manuscript so published becomes, not just possible, but inevitable. This is the power of the Author Mindset.

Design Your Morning Routine: Jump-Start Your Writing Success (Author Success Foundations Book 2)

https://ChristopherDiArmani.net/morning-routine

https://ChristopherDiArmani.net/morning-routine-workbook

There is no magic to writing a book. None. You take action, every single day, until your book is finished. You plan, schedule and execute the plan. You write.

If you are serious about finishing your manuscript, grab your notebook, a pen, and a cup of your favorite beverage, and join me at the kitchen table. We'll chat about habits, willpower and self-discipline. We'll discuss how the mind functions, what makes a habit stick, and how our willpower fades throughout the day. We'll talk about concrete steps to improve your self-discipline.

Then I'll ask you to complete a series of exercises. These exercises reveal, at a deep level, what's important to you - what you value most in life. This clarity of purpose allows you to create a morning routine designed to jump-start your daily writing output.

Author Focus: Develop Your Author Vision Statement and Laser-Focus Your Writing Career (Author Success Foundations Book 3)

https://ChristopherDiArmani.net/author-focus

https://ChristopherDiArmani.net/author-focus-workbook

Writing is easy. Finishing your book is easy, too.

Focus. Be diligent. Apply self-discipline and determination.

You already possess these qualities. This book would not appeal to you if you didn't.

Your author vision statement is an extraordinary targeting mechanism to guide you to your ultimate destination - the end of Publication Highway.

The exercises ahead serve one purpose - to focus your mind on what you value most - your published book.

Join me and map your personal journey down Publication Highway. Discover what you value most, not just in writing, but in your entire life.

Isn't your ideal future worth the time?

Prolific Author: The Step-by-Step Guide to Write More Words in Less Time and Finish Your Book Fast (Author Success Foundations 4)

https://ChristopherDiArmani.net/prolific-author

https://ChristopherDiArmani.net/prolific-author-workbook

The key to unlock your drive to succeed is knowing why you write. When you understand how your desire to write fulfills your core needs, you transform writing from a chore to be dreaded into the vision you were born to fulfill. Time set aside to write becomes as critical to your life as the food you eat and the water you drink.

If we believe success does not matter, neither does the road we travel to get there.

Success matters. The road you travel to achieve success matters more.

Your daily writing routine is the last piece of the puzzle to build a life focused on accomplishing your goal - a finished and published book.

Done is Better than Perfect: 7 Keys to Finish Writing Your Book Fast (Author Success Foundations 5)

https://ChristopherDiArmani.net/done-better-perfect

Give Up Your Perfectionism and Publish Your Book

The three fundamental truths of writing are:

1. Your book will never be perfect.
2. You cannot publish what you do not complete.
3. Done is better than perfect.

Learn how to finish your book easier, faster and better than you ever thought possible when you apply the Seven Keys of Writing Success.

Become Unstoppable: 7 Habits of Highly Successful Authors (Author Success Foundations Book 6)

https://ChristopherDiArmani.net/become-unstoppable

Success leaves clues.

Figure out what successful authors did to advance their careers, then do what they did. It's the most effective course of action. Simple concept, but we must do the work. You know, the hard part.

In the pages ahead I discuss how each habit works, as well as the lies we tell ourselves to rationalize our lack of forward progress. Finally, I shine the light of truth on the lies we tell ourselves and watch as they scurry away like little cockroaches.

Apply these principles to your life and you'll achieve their success. It's inevitable. All it takes is a pinch of perseverance, a dash of focus, and two cups of hard work.

I Don't Have Time To Write And Other Lies Writers Tell Themselves (Author Success Foundations Book 7)

https://ChristopherDiArmani.net/no-time-to-write

Stop Lying To Yourself.

In this installment of the Author Success Foundations series, I dissect seven lies writers tell ourselves and shine the light of truth upon each one.

Every falsehood obscures a truth we refuse to confront. The job of a writer, any writer, is to face our fears head on, protected by the body armor of honesty and integrity. Only then does the brilliance we etch on the page shine bright for the world to see.

Each delusion corrodes holes in our armor, holes the insidious demons of worry, self-doubt, procrastination and perfectionism slip through to poison us.

The Author Success Foundations series provides the tools and materials to patch those holes, to reinforce and strengthen our armor. The day of battle is here, and we must march ever forward. If we stop, even for a moment, our words shrink under the oppressive heat of our fears and we fail.

Step inside. Face your fears. Show these pathetic demons you cannot be cowed. Own your internal dialog and reshape it into a powerful engine, then use that power to drive down Publication Highway.

The Simple 3-Step Secret to Slaughter Writer's Block And Vanquish it Forever

https://ChristopherDiArmani.net/Writers-Block-Book

There is no more perfect Hell than one where I cannot write. You know that terror, too, don't you? That sense your last remaining creative spark abandoned you some time back. It's sickening.

Let me show you how to extricate yourself from that "perfect Hell" permanently.

TOP SECRET - Inspiration, Motivation and Encouragement - 701 Essential Quotes for Writers

https://ChristopherDiArmani.net/Top-Secret-Quotes

This compilation of 701 quotes delivers inspiration, motivation and encouragement on 39 aspects of writing and the writing life.

You will discover quotes to make you laugh and quotes to make you cry. Some are familiar, like old friends. Others you will meet for the first time. All have a common theme: The Writing Life.

When you need it most, you will find words of encouragement here.

Filming Police is Legal - How to Hold Police Accountable While Staying Out of Jail

I write about police issues regularly. I highlight good cops when I can, but I focus on the problems in our police forces with honesty, integrity and abuse. Every time news breaks about police seizing another citizen's camera or cell phone I receive the same question.

Christopher, is it legal to film police?

The unequivocal answer is a court-affirmed YES. It is legal to film police in every state in the United States of America and in every single province and territory of Canada. That YES comes with specific caveats for the audio portion of a recording depending upon your jurisdiction, and it is critical you know those caveats.

The purpose of this book is to educate mere citizens and police forces alike about the legality of the right of citizens to film police, along with an examination of the legal history supporting our legal right to do so.

https://ChristopherDiArmani.net/Filming-Police

Justin Trudeau - 47 Character-Revealing Quotes from Canada's 23rd Prime Minister and What They Mean for You

On October 19, 2015 Canadians elected their 23rd Prime Minister based on good looks, nice hair and a famous name.

They voted for style over substance.

Our 23rd Prime Minister's entire leadership experience consisted of teaching snowboarding lessons and high school drama. His management experience consisted of administering his trust fund and his ego.

Not a single thought was given to what he stood for, what his party stood for, or what he would actually do once elected to the highest office in the land. That bothered me. That bothered me so much I began to research his much-publicized missteps and that in turn revealed a disturbing pattern within Trudeau's numerous faux pas. That pattern is the focus of this book.

https://ChristopherDiArmani.net/Justin-Trudeau-Book-1

From Refugee to Cabinet Minister: Maryam Monsef's Meteoric Rise to Power and her Spectacular Fall From Grace

Maryam Monsef is the ultimate immigrant success story. She could not speak English when she arrived in Canada at age eleven. Two decades later she became Canada's first Muslim Cabinet Minister.

Maryam Monsef's story begins with her mother, a young Afghan widow who fled Afghanistan for Canada with her three young daughters in 1995. That widow spoke English but her three daughters did not. They brought something far more valuable to Canada: the unshakeable belief they could accomplish anything they wanted, so long as they worked hard.

It's no accident her belief in herself led Maryam Monsef to a Cabinet post. She worked hard to learn English and graduated from Trent University, an impossible accomplishment in her native Afghanistan.

Maryam Monsef became the unwitting scapegoat for Trudeau's broken promise on electoral reform, a promise he knew he would break by May 2016. Her birthplace controversy, her attempts to discredit and insult her electoral reform committee, combined with the Prime Minister's betrayal of her trust, sounded the death knell of her political career.

This, then, is the story of one young woman's meteoric rise to political power. It is also the story of that young woman's undoing at the hands of a narcissistic and self-serving celebrity feminist, Justin Trudeau.

https://ChristopherDiArmani.net/Maryam-Monsef-Book

Endnotes

1   Tracy, Brian. "No Excuses! The Power of Self-Discipline." Vanguard Press, 2011. Kindle Edition

2   Gillett, Rachel. "The best music to listen to for optimal productivity, according to science." Business Insider Inc., Jul. 24, 2015, http://www.businessinsider.com/the-best-music-for-productivity-2015-7. Accessed: Jan. 10, 2018.

3   Engel, Allison. "Studying for finals? Let classical music help." USC News, Dec. 5, 2014, https://news.usc.edu/71969/studying-for-finals-let-classical-music-help/. Accessed: Jan. 10, 2018.

4   Nelson, Brooke. "10 Wondrous Things That Happen to Your Body When You Listen to Classical Music." Reader's Digest, Undated, https://www.rd.com/health/wellness/classical-music-effects/. Accessed: Jan. 10, 2018.

5   Baker, Mitzi. "Music moves brain to pay attention, Stanford study finds." Stanford Medicine, Aug. 1, 2007, https://med.stanford.edu/news/all-news/2007/07/music-moves-brain-to-pay-attention-stanford-study-finds.html. Accessed: Jan. 10, 2018.

6   Padnani, Amisha. "The Power of Music, Tapped in a Cubicle." The New York Times Company, AUG. 11, 2012, http://www.nytimes.com/2012/08/12/jobs/how-music-can-improve-worker-productivity-workstation.html. Accessed: Jan. 10, 2018.

www.ingramcontent.com/pod-product-compliance
Lightning Source LLC
Chambersburg PA
CBHW070857050426
42453CB00012B/2251